365 REASONS TO BE PROUD

First published in Great Britain
in 2026 by Hamlyn, an imprint of
Octopus Publishing Group Ltd
Carmelite House
50 Victoria Embankment
London EC4Y 0DZ
www.octopusbooks.co.uk

An Hachette UK Company
www.hachette.co.uk

The authorized representative in the EEA
is Hachette Ireland, 8 Castlecourt Centre,
Dublin 15, D15 XTP3, Ireland
(email: info@hbgi.ie)

Text copyright © Octopus Publishing
Group Ltd 2026

Distributed in the US by
Hachette Book Group
1290 Avenue of the Americas,
4th and 5th Floors
New York, NY 10104

Distributed in Canada by
Canadian Manda Group
664 Annette St., Toronto,
Ontario, Canada M6S 2C8

All rights reserved. No part of this work
may be reproduced or utilized in any
form or by any means, electronic or
mechanical, including photocopying,
recording or by any information storage
and retrieval system, without the prior
written permission of the publisher.

Tim Leng asserts the moral right to be
identified as the author of this work.

ISBN: 978-0-60063-997-8
eISBN: 978-0-60063-998-5

A CIP catalogue record for this book
is available from the British Library.

Printed and bound in China.

10 9 8 7 6 5 4 3 2 1

Publisher: Lucy Pessell
Designers: Isobel Platt &
Kathrine Anderson
Compiling Editor: Tim Leng
Assistant Editor: Samina Rahman
Production Manager: Allison Gonsalves

365 REASONS TO BE PROUD

hamlyn

It's a noisy old world, isn't it?

Everyone thinks out loud. They type ferociously. The clamour builds, so voices have to yell, and opinions get more heated, and people disagree for the sake of disagreeing, and the firestorm blazes and the world spins hotter and faster and madder...

That's true for any subject. The argument would rage if we asked whether we should bring back Spangles. But when the subject matter is close to your heart, if it's an issue of sex or sexuality or gender or simply 'Can I wear that dress?' then those loud voices can hurt.

Welcome to a moment's peace.

This kind, beautiful book takes thoughts from people who've been there, people who've lived that life or watched that life closely, and have something to say about it. Not loudly, but wisely. It's a gorgeous collection, so well curated, and it's fun to think of all those quoted here in a great big out-and-proud dinner party. Marsha P Johnson and Lady Gaga singing a duet.

Tennessee Williams and Harvey Milk propping up the bar. Tove Jansson showing her latest story to George Michael. What a night that would be!

Well, thanks to Tim Leng, you can have that party whenever you want, in your own head. The words gathered here are clever, vital, funny, compassionate and true. A little gift to yourself every day of the year. Go on, have fun, you deserve it.

And yes. You look great in that dress!

Russell T Davies
July 2025

Darling, I want my gay rights now.

MARTHA P JOHNSON

PRIDE IS A PROTEST.

IT ALWAYS HAS BEEN

AND ALWAYS WILL BE.

I'm not missing a moment of this – it's the revolution!

SYLVIA RIVERA

BE A KING. BE A QUEEN. BE ANYTHING IN-BETWEEN.

Gender is a galaxy! You're a miraculous embodiment of belonging, possibility and wonder! There's nobody like you in the universe – that's exactly why you belong.

SAMANTHA RISE

TODAY IS AN AWFULLY GOOD DAY TO BE QUEER.

MY FEMININITY MAKES ME A BETTER MAN.

MARS WRIGHT

THERE ARE PLENTY OF COLOURS IN THE RAINBOW – FIND YOUR PLACE ON IT.

What I liked about the rainbow is that it fits all of us. It's all the colours. It represents all the genders. It represents all the races. It's the rainbow of humanity.

GILBERT BAKER

COMING OUT MIGHT BE ONE OF THE HARDEST THINGS YOU EVER DO... BUT IT CAN ALSO BE ONE OF THE MOST LIBERATING.

Personally, coming out was one of the most important things I've ever done, lifting from my shoulders the millstone of lies that I hadn't even realized I was carrying.

SIR IAN McKELLEN

Find your tribe and surround yourself with the people that make your heart sing.

Use the pronouns that define YOU.

BE MASC, BE FEM, BE ANDROGYNOUS, BE WHATEVER YOU WANT TO BE. JUST BE BRILLIANTLY, UNIQUELY YOU.

GENDER IS A SPECTRUM, NOT FIXED LINES DRAWN IN THE SAND.

I'm a 'they', so what?

FOXY FOX

If a transvestite doesn't say I'm gay and I'm proud and I'm a transvestite, then nobody else is going to hop up there and say I'm gay and I'm proud and I'm a transvestite for them.

MARSHA P JOHNSON

EMBRACE EVERYONE, NO MATTER THE WAY THEY DRESS, ACT OR TALK.

TOGETHER WE'RE STRONGER.

WE WILL NOT WIN OUR RIGHTS BY STAYING QUIETLY IN OUR CLOSETS.

HARVEY MILK

Every day is just another opportunity to be fabulous.

CHIN UP, IT'S TIME TO RIDE THAT IMAGINARY UNICORN INTO BATTLE.

If homosexuality is a disease, let's all call in queer to work: 'Hello. Can't work today, still queer.'

ROBIN TYLER

BE UNAPOLOGETICALLY AMAZING.

We live in a world that has always been biologically and culturally sex/gender diverse. Rise up and celebrate this birthright.

JENN BURLETON

> You're never alone among like-minded people.

Love him and let him love you. Do you think anything else under heaven really matters?

JAMES BALDWIN

LET LOVE SHINE ALWAYS

YOU DESERVE THE WORLD.

THERE'S MAGIC IN YOU – LET EVERYONE SEE IT.

Everything about us, about you, is a revolution: existing, just being together, finding joy, being seen even in the smallest 'I love your hair' or 'that pin/button/patch is so cool' moments. So keep doing that: exist, see each other, pick up all the joy you can find.

WULF ROBY

IT'S YOUR RIGHT TO BE SEEN, HEARD AND VALUED.

SING LOUD AND DANCE YOUR ASS OFF.

Always be a first-rate version of yourself, instead of a second-rate version of somebody else.

JUDY GARLAND

A SLAY A DAY KEEPS THE HOMOPHOBES AWAY.

Keep doing it with grace. Keep doing it with love. Don't ever stop your motivation, your momentum on changing the world and changing humans hearts. Please don't be in fear. Be you.

MICHAELA JAÉ RODRIGUEZ

Never be afraid to embrace new looks.

ONE OF THE MOST IMPORTANT THINGS YOU CAN DO IS BE VISIBLE.

Never be bullied into silence. Never allow yourself to be made a victim. Accept no one's definition of your life, but define yourself.

HARVEY FIERSTEIN

LIVE THE LIFE YOU'VE ALWAYS IMAGINED.

NOT EVERYONE WILL UNDERSTAND YOU, AND THAT'S OK. DON'T EVER LET THEM MAKE YOU DOUBT YOURSELF.

Why is it that, as a culture, we are more comfortable seeing two men holding guns than holding hands?

ERNEST J GAINES

GILBERT BAKER GAVE US OUR FIRST RAINBOW – SAY A THANK YOU FOR THIS ICONIC FLAG EVERY TIME YOU WAVE IT.

SURE, JAN.

To be yourself is truly a revolutionary act, and I think more and more people should try it, because it's gotten me a pretty cool life.

LENA WAITHE

Wear fabulous clothes that make you feel empowered.

Learn the colours of the flag, what they mean, who they represent and the story they tell.

Don't be afraid. Don't be ashamed. Don't ever apologise for your sexuality. Just be You.

SONYA DEVILLE

We're here, we've always been here, and we will always be here.

If I wait for someone else to validate my existence, it will mean that I'm shortchanging myself.

ZANELE MUHOLI

LEARN THE STORY OF THE PEOPLE WHO CAME BEFORE YOU AND FOUGHT FOR YOUR RIGHTS...

...and keep fighting for the people that will follow you.

MEMBERS OF OUR COMMUNITY ARE EVERYWHERE YOU LOOK. YOU ARE NEVER ALONE.

Each and every one of you is here for a divine purpose. You might not see it right now but you are here for a divine purpose and so you have to survive. You have to survive.

LAVERNE COX

IT'S NEVER OVER UNTIL WE HAVE EQUALITY FOR ALL.

Equality is not a pie; there is more than enough for everyone.

CHARLOTTE CLYMER

GO TO A PRIDE EVENT AND EXPERIENCE THE JOY OF BEING AMONG SO MANY DIVERSE MEMBERS OF OUR COMMUNITY.

Whether it's on a pin, a hat, or emblazoned on your T-shirt, share your rainbow with pride.

Every single American — gay, straight, lesbian, bisexual, transgender — every single American deserves to be treated equally in the eyes of the law and in the eyes of our society. It's a pretty simple proposition.

PRESIDENT BARACK OBAMA

> This is your story to write, fill it with all the plot twists you want.

You have to go the way your blood beats. If you don't live the only life you have, you won't live some other life – you won't live any life at all.

JAMES BALDWIN

IT'S NOT
A CLICHÉ:
LOVE IS LOVE.

FIND THE ALLIES WHO CHAMPION YOU AND FIGHT YOUR CORNER.

The tiniest intentional acts of caring for each other, fuelled by rage against a system that kills us, fosters communities of Stubborn Survivors. See each other. Hold each other. Together We THRIVE.

RYDER FOX

IT WON'T ALWAYS BE EASY, BUT STAY YOUR COURSE.

FEEL PRIDE IN THE INCREDIBLE VIBRANCY OF THE PEOPLE WHO MAKE UP OUR COMMUNITY.

Gender diversity is part of our reality. The sooner we can hold space for the complexity of this, the closer we will come to a future that celebrates all genders and sexualities, and cares for and protects all bodies.

SHANNON MAY POWELL

ASK YOURSELF: HOW CAN I MAKE A DIFFERENCE?

How can I explain how everything has changed since I met you! Every tone is more vivid, every colour cleaner, all my perceptions are sharper – my happiness is stronger, my despair more powerful.

TOVE JANSSON

Hold hands with the person you love, proudly, defiantly, at every opportunity.

Love is a flower; you've got to let it grow.

JOHN LENNON

EVERY DAY IS AN OPPORTUNITY TO WALK AN IMAGINARY RED CARPET.

There may be a compulsion to hide some aspects of yourself: Don't!

I want back the years I worried about my own authenticity. Turns out, confidently being yourself makes you a source of strength for other people.

EVERETT MAROON

STRAIGHTEN YOUR CROWN AND SHOW THE WORLD HOW INCREDIBLE YOU ARE.

There is nothing more wonderful than being out, proud and authentically you.

We can climb mountains with self-love. I want to make sure that any young person, or anyone, really, who is looking up to me...that they see no shame, that they see pride, and that I'm truly unabashed about the person that I am.

SAMIRA WILEY

LOOK FOR THE RAINBOWS EVERYWHERE.

BE THE REASON SOMEONE FEELS ABLE TO SHOW THEIR TRUE COLOURS WITH PRIDE.

My silences had not protected me. Your silence will not protect you.

AUDRE LORDE

We all have a role to play in making this world a better place for everyone.

So many people in this community have remarkable stories to tell: listen to them.

What is straight? A line can be straight, or a street, but the human heart, oh, no, it's curved like a road through mountains.

TENNESSEE WILLIAMS

HE, SHE, THEY, THEM – IT'S NOT DIFFICULT TO RESPECT PEOPLE'S PRONOUNS.

Pay it no mind.

MARTHA P JOHNSON

BE UNITED IN PRIDE.

EXPLORE THE HISTORY OF THE RAINBOW FLAG AND LEARN HOW IT HAS CHANGED WITH THE TIMES.

I'M NOT GAY, ALTHOUGH I WISH I WERE, JUST TO PISS OFF HOMOPHOBES.

KURT COBAIN

Beyond the rainbow there are so many other flags. Lesbian, bi, trans, gender fluid, intersex – even straight ally. Read about them and perhaps you'll find a new one to embrace.

Each trans and nonbinary person is like a unique and beautiful snowflake. Some people are more comfortable in their body and don't need surgery or hormone therapy, and others do. No one way is right or wrong, and what you're feeling is your gender dysphoria.

TOBLY McSMITH

Be someone's fabulous
gay best friend.

Being gay is like being left-handed; some people are, most people aren't, and nobody really knows exactly why. It's not right or wrong. It's just one of the many natural ways to be. The world works best when everyone gets to live as they truly are. So if you ever feel out of place, remember: you're not broken, you're just beautifully different, and that's something the world needs.

JODIE FOSTER

Gay. Straight. Somewhere in between or whatever you want to be. We're all just human beings who love and want to be loved.

It always seemed to me a bit pointless to disapprove of homosexuality. It's like disapproving of rain.

FRANCIS MAUDE

BEING GAY IS GREAT. WHY WOULD YOU WANT TO BE ANY OTHER WAY?

Radiate positivity and acceptance.

I would advise any gay person that being out in the real sense... can never happen too soon.

GEORGE MICHAEL

SHINE BRIGHTER EACH AND EVERY DAY.

Coming out will change you forever – like a caterpillar turning into a butterfly you become the beautiful thing you were always destined to be.

I am a strong, Black, lesbian woman. Every single time I say it, I feel so much better.

BRITTNEY GRINER

L before the G to recognize everything the lesbian community did for gay men during the AIDS crisis of the 1980s.

SPRINKLE A LITTLE QUEER MAGIC EVERY DAY.

SOUNDS GAY, I'M IN.

Do not grow old, no matter how long you live. Never cease to stand like curious children before the great mystery into which we were born.

ALBERT EINSTEIN

Show courage and determination in promoting change.

BE GAY, DO CRIME.

I AM THE WAY I AM BECAUSE NOBODY COULD CONVINCE ME TO BE OTHERWISE.

NEELI CHERKOVSKI

ACCEPT EVERYONE'S UNIQUENESS.

We love because it's the
only true adventure.

NIKKI GIOVANNI

It's OK if you don't feel ready to come out right now – take the time you need to feel comfortable in your own skin.

I just wish more of my fellow queers would come out sometimes. It's nice out here, you know?

ELTON JOHN

Be kind to others – you never know what they're going through.

> COMING OUT IS SOMETHING YOU WILL NEVER FORGET AND NEVER REGRET.

I've always been Sarah. My gender identity has always existed. I've always been a woman. Gay people aren't straight before they come out as gay, and transgender people are who they are before they come out and transition.

SARAH McBRIDE

DON'T LET ANYONE TELL YOU WHO YOU ARE – YOU ARE YOU AND NO ONE CAN CHANGE THAT.

You are everything to someone.

I hate the word homophobia. It's not a phobia. You're not scared. You're an asshole.

PRIDE COMES FROM WITHIN. LET IT RADIATE OUT.

POSITIVE VIBES ONLY.

I want people to walk around delusional about how great they can be – and then to fight so hard for it every day that the lie becomes the truth.

LADY GAGA

The first thing you should do every morning is sit up in bed and remind yourself how amazing you are.

Whoever you are and whatever you do, be in love.

RUMI

BE A RAY OF SUNSHINE IN A SKY OF CLOUDS.

Ain't no rainbow without the rain.
Weather any storm, it will pass.

It's a strange lesson to learn in life that your differences, the things that make you feel uncomfortable about yourself, are what will help you to grow into who you are. Those are your gifts.

CYNDI LAUPER

Your feelings are valid, don't let anyone tell you otherwise.

We have to be visible. We should not be ashamed of who we are.

SYLVIA RIVERA

DON'T QUESTION YOURSELF, JUST BE COMFORTABLE WITH WHO YOU ARE.

One life, live it well.

When you show up as your authentic self, whatever that may be, you allow others to do the same, creating the world we all deserve.

SHANNA KATZ KATTARI

BE TRUE TO YOURSELF.

Gender is not what people look like to other people; it is what we know ourselves to be. No one else should be able to tell you who you are; that's for you to decide...Man and woman are two of many – stars in a constellation that do not compete but amplify one another's shine.

ALOK VAID-MENON

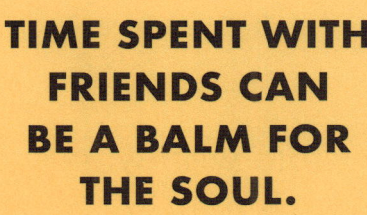

TIME SPENT WITH FRIENDS CAN BE A BALM FOR THE SOUL.

DON'T HOLD ON TO
ANY SHAME OR FEAR.
LET THAT SHIT GO.

There's nothing wrong with you. There's a lot wrong with the world you live in.

CHRIS COLFER

Be comfortable with who you are and never compare yourself to others.

LIVE LIFE AT YOUR OWN PACE.

I am tired of hiding and I am tired of lying by omission.

ELLIOT PAGE

Be bold, fierce, magical and beautiful.

SOME OF US NEED TIME TO BECOME THE PERSON WE'RE DESTINED TO BE – TRUST YOURSELF.

Trans people are extraordinary, strong, intelligent, persistent and resilient. We have to be. And we will not stand for the picking and choosing of rights. We still have hope.

GRACE DOLAN-SANDRINO

Nobody has the right to question your identity – that's your story to tell.

YOU DIDN'T CHOOSE TO BE QUEER, BUT IT'S A BEAUTIFUL GIFT THAT LOOKS GOOD ON YOU.

Not everyone will understand your journey. That's OK. You are here to live your life, not to make everyone understand.

BANKSY

Be kind to yourself, always and unconditionally.

WE'RE HERE, WE'RE QUEER, WE WILL NOT LIVE IN FEAR.

When an individual is protesting society's refusal to acknowledge his dignity as a human being, his very act of protest confers dignity on him.

BAYARD RUSTIN

YOU DESERVE TO LIVE THE LIFE YOU WANT.

Identity is a fluid concept. It evolves and grows with us.

LANA WACHOWSKI

THE ROAD MIGHT SOMETIMES FEEL LONELY, BUT THERE ARE ALWAYS FELLOW TRAVELLERS TO HELP YOU ON YOUR JOURNEY.

Be flirty, be camp, be shy, be outrageous, just let the real you shine.

There's power in being seen.
By living authentically and
fully as ourselves, we're also
ensuring that those who need
to see someone like us, can.

ANDY DURAN

LOVE. AIN'T IT GRAND?

YOU NEVER KNOW WHO YOU'RE
GOING TO FALL FOR, BUT WHEN
YOU MEET THAT PERSON
LET IT BE THE THING GREAT
SONGS ARE WRITTEN ABOUT.

I live proudly in a body of my own design. I defend my right to be complex.

LESLIE FEINBERG

FALL IN LOVE

WITH BEING QUEER.

DON'T CHANGE WHO YOU ARE TO MEET THE NARROW STANDARDS OF OTHERS.

Celebrate our community at every opportunity.

Hate never wins out in the end. It instead goes always to its lonely, dusty end.

GEORGE TAKEI

TAKE PART IN A PRIDE MARCH AT LEAST ONCE IN YOUR LIFE.

This community has fought and continues to fight a war of acceptance, a war of tolerance and the most relentless bravery. You are the definition of courage, do you know that?

LADY GAGA

Enjoy the party atmosphere of Pride, but never forget why we still need it.

You don't need to be perfect; we're all a work in progress.

The pressures on LGBTQ teens can be overwhelming – to keep secrets, tell lies, deny who you are, and try to be who you're not. Remember: you are special and worth being cared about, loved, and accepted just as you are. Never let anyone convince you otherwise.

ALEX SANCHEZ

Allies sharing Pride flags is a sign of solidarity that should make your heart sing.

DAY BY DAY, LITTLE BY LITTLE, WE'RE ALL WORKING TO MAKE THIS WORLD A BETTER PLACE FOR EVERYONE.

It's important to protect people and human beings, especially those that are simply asking for the right to exist in the bodies that belong to them and in the world that they never asked to be brought into.

PEDRO PASCAL

TELL YOUR STORY AND LISTEN TO THE STORIES OF OTHERS.

LABELS DON'T APPLY.

Owning our story and loving ourselves through that process is the bravest thing we'll ever do.

BRENÉ BROWN

OFFER HELP TO MEMBERS OF OUR COMMUNITY WHEN THEY FACE TOUGH TIMES.

PAY KINDNESS FORWARD.

What would you be like if you were the only person in the world? If you want to be truly happy you must be that person.

QUENTIN CRISP

Read about the AIDS Memorial Quilt and discover the stories of those we've lost.

CELEBRATE QUEER WRITERS AND ARTISTS.

I've never been interested in being invisible and erased.

LAVERNE COX

Take your straight friends to queer spaces – they'll have a great time and develop a deeper understanding of your experience.

CHAMPION QUEER-OWNED BUSINESSES.

Hell hath no fury like a drag queen scorned.

SYLVIA RIVERA

Explore the history of the LGBTQIA+ experience all the way back to ancient times and be proud of the generations who lived long before you.

Anyone who feels shy or uncomfortable about their sexuality should celebrate and be confident and be happy. It's a lovely, ordinary, normal thing.

DAME CAROL ANN DUFFY

Search online for queer couples of decades past and feel pride in the happy smiling faces looking back at you from vintage photographs.

LIFT OTHERS WITH YOUR WORDS AND SUPPORT THEM WITH YOUR ACTIONS.

Being gay is not a choice, but loving and respecting people is.

ELTON JOHN

BE PATIENT WITH THOSE WHO DON'T UNDERSTAND YOUR EXPERIENCE, AND EXPLAIN WHY IT MATTERS.

CHALLENGE HATE WHEREVER YOU FIND IT.

For me, the transgender thing is the reality of my life. It's the reality of my existence and it's something that I've come to believe is beautiful about me.

LAVERNE COX

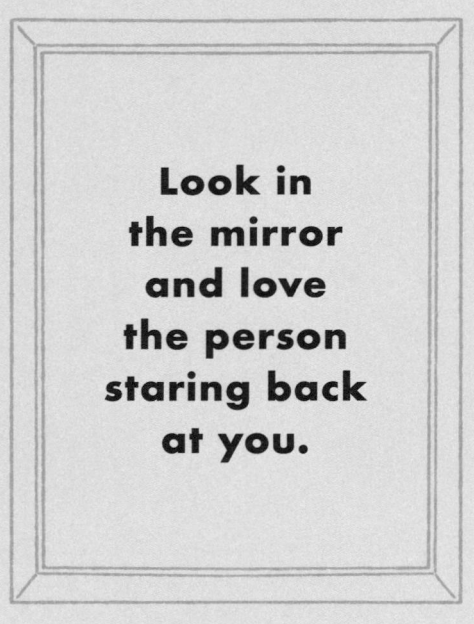

Look in the mirror and love the person staring back at you.

LOVE, HAPPINESS AND RESPECT COST NOTHING – SHARE THEM EVERYWHERE YOU GO.

LOVE HAS NO BOUNDARIES.

THIS AMAZING COMMUNITY ACCEPTS EVERYONE.

DIGNITY, EQUALITY, AND JUSTICE ARE FUNDAMENTAL TO ENSURING THAT ALL LGBTQIA+ PEOPLE FEEL SAFE AND PROTECTED.

PRESIDENT BARACK OBAMA

Being a human is hard work, but it's easier to carry that load together. Keep showing up and extending grace for yourself and others.

MX PUCKS A'PLENTY

YOU DON'T NEED ANYONE'S PERMISSION TO LIVE YOUR LIFE YOUR WAY.

Stand up and be counted.

Being born gay, Black and female is not a revolutionary act. Being proud to be a gay, Black female is.

LENA WAITHE

NO ONE EVER CHANGED THE WORLD BY BEING SHY AND RETIRING.

My mother took me to a psychiatrist when I was fifteen because she thought I was a latent homosexual. There was nothing latent about it.

AMANDA BEARSE

FALL IN LOVE WITH BEING IN LOVE.

You deserve every happiness.

All of us are put in boxes by our family, by our religion, by our society, our moment in history, even our own bodies. Some people have the courage to break free.

GEENA ROCERO

Take big steps, not baby steps.

Somehow, someway, you will make a difference.

EVERYTHING WILL BE OK.

Now we know that queer people and trans people are magic. So many kinds of magic and so many kinds of normal.

JOEY SOLOWAY

The next time someone asks you why LGBT Pride marches exist or why Gay Pride Month is June tell them "A bisexual woman named Brenda Howard thought it should be."

BRENDA HOWARD

BE WEIRD,

BE WONDERFUL,

BE BRILLIANT

AND BRAVE.

**Different is just different,
there's nothing wrong with it.**

To LGBT men and women worldwide, let me say this: wherever you live and whatever the circumstances of your life, whether you are connected to a network of support or feel isolated and vulnerable, please know that you are not alone.

HILLARY CLINTON

SAY IT LOUD: THIS IS WHO I AM.

BE A SOURCE OF INSPIRATION AT EVERY OPPORTUNITY.

Nothing here is promised, not one day... Love is love is love is love is love is love is love is love cannot be killed or swept aside... fill the world with music, love and pride.

LIN-MANUEL MIRANDA

Queer culture has given us so much beautiful art, literature, music and entertainment.

We are a community of world-changing creativity.

GIVE NO F*CKS.

When you become the image of your own imagination, it's the most powerful thing you could ever do.

RUPAUL

SURROUND YOURSELF
WITH LOVE, LAUGHTER
AND POSITIVITY.

IT DOESN'T ALWAYS HAVE TO BE YES OR NO, BLACK OR WHITE – THERE'S WONDER TO BE FOUND IN THE SPACES BETWEEN.

Celebrate how far you've come.

LIVE YOUR LIFE FABULOUSLY.

I've just never talked about it. But it's so liberating. It was interesting to be coming to have a conversation that I was always afraid to have. This is my coming out ball. I've been dying to do this.

SEAN MAHER

TO LOVE AND BE LOVED, THAT'S ALL WE ASK.

IT'S NOT A PHASE.

You are who you are. No one can tell you who you are but you. Whoever you know yourself to be, you are right.

MAYBE BURKE

ALWAYS BE TRUE TO YOURSELF.

Putting yourself out there is hard, but it's so worth it. I don't think anyone who has ever spoken out, or stood up or had a brave moment, has regretted it. It's empowering and confidence-building and inspiring. Not only to other people, but to yourself.

MEGAN RAPINOE

Being queer isn't always easy, but it's always worth the effort.

THE FUTURE IS INCLUSIVE.

There is no debate to argue here. Trans people have been here forever and aren't going anywhere. There is no ideology here. It's simple. Trans rights are human rights. Anything stating the contrary is wrong.

JAMIE LEE CURTIS

PROTECT THE DOLLS.

NEVER DOUBT YOUR POTENTIAL.

**KEEPING GOING,
KEEP GROWING.**

**Be nice,
do good things.**

You've got a huge personality; put it out there for everyone to see.

VIVA LA GAYS!

Always go a little further into the water than you feel you're capable of being in. Go a little bit out of your depth. And when you don't feel that your feet are quite touching the bottom, you're just about in the right place to do something exciting.

DAVID BOWIE

Love fully and unconditionally.

ACCEPT EVERYONE, WHATEVER THEIR STORY OR WHEREVER THEY COME FROM.

Make your world a magical place.

There's no right or wrong way to be gay. No right or wrong way to come out. It's your journey, do it the way you wanna do it.

TAN FRANCE

BE GOOD – AND IF YOU CAN'T BE GOOD BE CAREFUL.

Now is the time to speak up.

FIND LOVE IN EVERYTHING YOU DO.

A sure sign of a good time is still finding glitter days after the event.

I once worried that there was no place for trans people like me to participate in any way in our politics. Since coming out, though, I've seen that change is possible and I've learned that the only things that are truly impossible are the things we don't try. You can run, you can win and you can serve.

SARAH McBRIDE

BE FIERCE, FEARLESS AND FABULOUS.

EVERYONE IS WELCOME.

TIME TO SPARKLE.

So let me be clear: I'm proud to be gay, and I consider being gay among the greatest gifts God has given me.

TIM COOK

SPEAK YOUR TRUTH.

FIND YOUR PLACE.

LIVE LIFE WELL.

Being gay isn't something in and of itself that's a virtue any more than being straight is, but the attributes that gay people develop as a result of being gay – mainly empathy toward other people, and compassion and tolerance — those are things to be proud of.

ANDREW SCOTT

Never miss an opportunity to tell your queer friends how proud you are of them.

THERE WILL ALWAYS BE SOMEONE BY YOUR SIDE, ROOTING FOR YOU.

Tell your stories. Often and loudly. We need to hear you, and you need to be heard. Tell your stories. Someone is listening. I promise.

TONY AMATO

Revel in the happiness you feel when you're with the people you love.

YOUR POTENTIAL IS LIMITLESS.

Never fail to show wonder at the remarkable person you are.

We deserve to experience love fully, equally, without shame and without compromise.

ELLIOT PAGE

LET THE COMMUNITY THAT SURROUNDS YOU INSPIRE YOU EVERY DAY.

WE'RE POWERFUL ALONE BUT UNSTOPPABLE TOGETHER.

Celebrate diversity in all its many wonderful forms.

FORGE YOUR OWN PATH WITH DEFIANCE.

Take pride in yourself and the people around you.

The beauty of standing up for your rights is others see you standing and stand up as well.

CASSANDRA DUFFY

Don't fear the things that make us different – celebrate them.

IF BAD TIMES COME,

GOOD TIMES

WILL FOLLOW.

Live life by your own set of fabulous rules.

CHERISH EVERY SECOND OF EVERY DAY, AND MAKE THEM ALL COUNT.

Be an extraordinary person in an ordinary world.

One person can light the spark that changes the world.

How many years has it taken people to realize that we are all brothers and sisters and human beings in the human race?

MARSHA P JOHNSON

I'm nonbinary, so I just don't see myself as a woman, solely. I feel all of my energy. I feel like God is so much bigger than the 'he' or the 'she.' If I am from God, I am everything.

JANELLE MONÁE

FEEL GOOD ABOUT YOURSELF, AND HELP OTHERS FEEL THE SAME.

Hang a flag in your window and show the world your true colours.

Don't change yourself in an effort to please others.

Being born between two cultures and coming to terms with your queerness sounded a little bit similar. Identities and self-acceptance shift in a world where you are not the default.

ELLIE FREEMAN

NEVER BE AFRAID OF WANTING TO BE WHO YOU TRULY ARE.

TREASURE THE THINGS THAT MAKE YOU HAPPY AND THE PEOPLE WHO MAKE YOU SMILE.

It is absolutely imperative that every human being's freedom and human rights are respected, all over the world.

JÓHANNA SIGURÐARDÓTTIR

CHOOSE LOVE.

DON'T BE AFRAID TO TAKE A LITTLE LEAP OF RAINBOW-POWERED FAITH NOW AND AGAIN.

I am the love that dare
not speak its name.

LORD ALFRED DOUGLAS

BE THE RAY OF SUNLIGHT THAT BRIGHTENS SOMEONE'S DAY.

My struggle has allowed me to transcend that sense of shame and stigma identified with my being a Black gay man. Having come through the fire, they can't touch me.

MARLON RIGGS

> Have you ever realized how lucky this world is to have you in it?

You aren't hard to love (your existence is a blessing). Your pronouns (or if you don't use them) aren't a burden. You're a dream fulfilled.

JULIÁN JAMAICA SOTO

LIVE FREELY, LOVE FIERCELY.

Take a compliment, pay a compliment.

People will stare. Make it worth their while.

HARRY WINSTON

We are all flawed, messy human beings, and that's OK.

BE STRONG, SASSY AND A LITTLE BAD ASS-Y.

Openness may not completely disarm prejudice, but it's a good place to start.

JASON COLLINS

The world isn't always a kind place, so do your bit to make it a better place.

THERE'S A PLACE FOR US ALL IN THIS WORLD.

Fears are not facts.

CHAZ BONO

WHATEVER LIFE THROWS AT YOU, KNOW YOU HAVE THE STRENGTH TO SEE IT THROUGH.

YOU ARE AN AMAZING BUNDLE OF LIMITLESS POTENTIAL.

Being transgender gives me my personality.

JAZZ JENNINGS

NEVER LET ANYONE TELL YOU THAT YOU CAN'T.

One person can make a difference.

You can do anything if you put your mind to it.

Every gay and lesbian person who has been lucky enough to survive the turmoil of growing up is a survivor. Survivors always have an obligation to those who will face the same challenges.

BOB PARRIS

Sing loud, even if you don't know the words.

On my darkest days, I wear my brightest colours.

CYNDI LAUPER

CHERISH EVERY MOMENT.

Never hold back from telling people how much they mean to you.

Love, happiness, kindness – there can never be enough of these things in the world.

I've had to go against all kinds of people through the years just to be myself. I think everybody should be allowed to be who they are, and to love who they love.

DOLLY PARTON

Strive to make a positive impact on someone's life each and every day.

Somebody, your father or mine, should have told us that not many people have ever died of love. But multitudes have perished, and are perishing every hour – and in the oddest places! – for the lack of it.

JAMES BALDWIN

GO OUT AND RANDOMLY
TELL SOMEONE HOW AMAZING
THEY LOOK TODAY.

**RADIATE POSITIVITY LIKE
YOU'RE THE GODDAMNED SUN.**

You can live in this light of the truth. It's totally liberating. You don't have to live a lie.

GILBERT BAKER

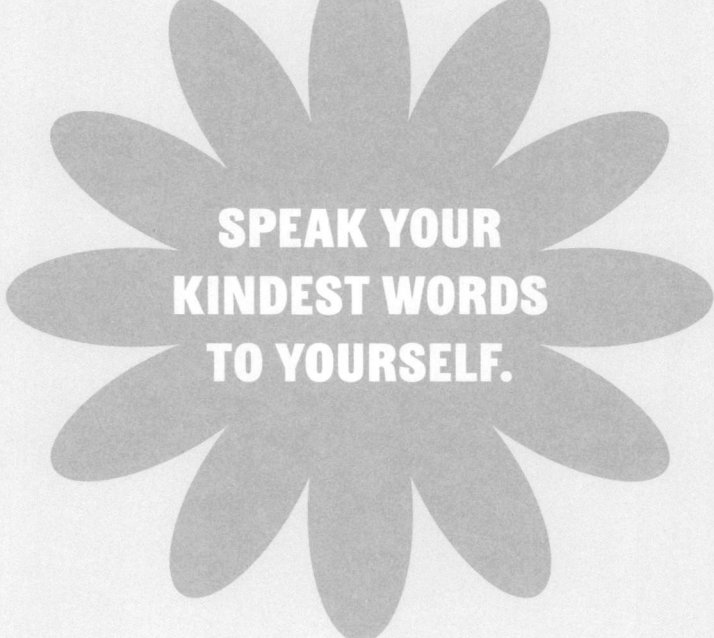

SPEAK YOUR KINDEST WORDS TO YOURSELF.

Time spent with people who make you laugh and feel loved is never wasted time.

I never say "trans but," always "trans and." Because it's like, no, I don't hide who I am. People know exactly who I am here.

DANICA ROEM

THERE ARE SO MANY INCREDIBLE DAYS STILL TO COME.

You have nothing to prove.

**Celebrate your queerness
not just in Pride month,
but every damn day.**

FOLLOW YOUR OWN HAPPINESS.

Pride is power.

Being transgender isn't a medical transition. It's a process of learning to love yourself for who you are.

JAZZ JENNINGS

PROTECT TRANS KIDS.

HATE TO BREAK IT TO THE HOMOPHOBES, BUT WE'RE NOT GOING ANYWHERE.

Never give up on living your true self, no matter how hard it is.

CAROLINE COSSEY

> There isn't a trans moment. It's just a presence where there was an absence. We deserve so much more.
>
> HARI NEF

TRANS WOMEN ARE WOMEN, TRANS MEN ARE MEN: DEAL WITH IT.

> Do I feel like a man or a woman? And the answer is: I feel happy.
>
> ABIGAIL THORNE

Being bi doesn't mean you have to explain who you fall in love with.

Who cares who you fall for, as long as they make you smile.

What is new is not bisexuality, but rather the widening of our awareness and acceptance of human capacities for sexual love.

MARGARET MEAD

THE AUTHENTIC YOU WILL ATTRACT AMAZING PEOPLE.

Every single lesbian and transgender woman is a woman.

PATRICIA ARQUETTE

PANSEXUAL AND DAMN PROUD OF IT.

Be that gay best friend that makes everyone's life better.

It is time that we all perceive gender as a spectrum instead of two sets of opposing ideals.

EMMA WATSON

YOU'RE DOING YOUR BEST AND THAT'S MORE THAN ENOUGH.

IF YOU'RE READING THIS, KNOW THAT YOU'RE LOVED.

For a lot of my life, I was judged for my gender representation or my sexual orientation, or what people assumed of me; and every single time my goal has been to combat that and show my greatness.

TAYLOR SMALL

BE BRILLIANTLY,

BEAUTIFULLY,

BOLDLY BISEXUAL.

 **EVERY ONE OF US DESERVES TO FEEL SAFE.**

If you are not personally free to be yourself in that most important of all human activities – the expression of love – then life itself loses its meaning.

HARVEY MILK

I HOPE YOU LOOK AT YOURSELF AND KNOW JUST HOW INCREDIBLE YOU ARE.

Say it a bit louder for those at the back: BEING GAY IS GREAT.

YOU'RE MORE POWERFUL, MORE POTENT, MORE BRAVE THAN YOU EVER GIVE YOURSELF CREDIT FOR.

You know, gay, lesbian, bisexual, transgender – people are people.

JUDITH LIGHT

Males do not represent two discrete populations, heterosexual and homosexual. The world is not to be divided into sheeps and goats. Not all things are black nor all things white. It is a fundamental of taxonomy that nature rarely deals with discrete categories. Only the human mind invents categories and tries to force facts into separated pigeon-holes. The living world is a continuum in each and every one of its aspects. The sooner we learn this concerning human sexual behaviour the sooner we shall reach a sound understanding of the realities of sex.

ALFRED KINSEY

Queer is your superpower.

LACONIC, IRONIC, 100% ICONIC.

There are worse things in the world than a boy who likes to kiss other boys.

BENJAMIN ALIRE SÁENZ

No judgement
(just the occasional shady look).

The best thing about being a girl is, now I don't have to pretend to be a boy.

AVERY JACKSON

Dance like no one is watching? Shake your ass and make it a PERFORMANCE.

WE CAN CHANGE THIS WORLD.

Let's wrap this planet
in a rainbow.

I know I'm perfectly as capable of being swayed by a girl as by a boy. More and more people feel that way, and I don't see why I shouldn't.

DUSTY SPRINGFIELD

HAVE A LITTLE

SASHAY EVERY DAY.

We carry inside us the wonders
we seek outside us.

RUMI

**Imagine a day when
everyone is treated equally
with love and respect...**

**...Then go out and
make it a reality.**

MAY YOU THRIVE IN
EVERYTHING YOU DO.

More people need to find the inspiration, the courage, to just speak up, because when the riot gets too loud, no matter how hard whoever tries, it's not possible to calm it. When the fire's too big, you can't have enough water to put it down.

EMMIE AMERICA

No pride for some of us without liberation for all of us.

MARSHA P JOHNSON

BE PROUD, ALWAYS.